WHEN I FEEL ANGRY

Amy Beattie

Enslow Publishing
101 W. 23rd Street
Suite 240
New York, NY 10011
USA

enslow.com

Published in 2020 by Enslow Publishing, LLC
101 W. 23rd Street, Suite 240, New York, NY 10011

Library of Congress Cataloging-in-Publication Data

Names: Beattie, Amy, author.
Title: When I feel angry / Amy Beattie.
Description: New York : Enslow Publishing, 2020 | Series: My feelings |
  Includes bibliographical references and index. | Audience: Grades K–2.
Identifiers: LCCN 2019009110| ISBN 9781978511620 (library bound) | ISBN
  9781978511590 (pbk.) | ISBN 9781978511606 (6 pack)
Subjects: LCSH: Anger.
Classification: LCC BF575.A5 B423 2019 | DDC 152.4/7—dc23
LC record available at https://lccn.loc.gov/2019009110

Printed in the United States of America

To Our Readers: We have done our best to make sure all websites in this book were active and appropriate when we went to press. However, the author and the publisher have no control over and assume no liability for the material available on those websites or on any websites they may link to. Any comments or suggestions can be sent by email to customerservice@enslow.com.

Contents

I feel angry when I fight with my sister.

We want to watch different shows. We yell at each other.

Our grandpa reminds us to use our inside voices. He reads me a story. My sister watches her show.

We agree to take turns picking shows. We promise Grandpa we will not shout anymore.

I feel angry when I lose at board games.

My babysitter always beats me at this
game. It is not fair. I want to throw the
pieces on the floor.

I take a deep breath. My babysitter is much better at the game than I am. She has played it a lot more.

If I **practice**, maybe I can win more often!

I feel angry when I drop a plate. It breaks into lots of little pieces.

I want to glue it back together. My mommy says there will be too many holes. We have lots of other plates.

I feel angry when I get sick. I cannot go to my friend's **superhero** birthday party.

My mom says my friend and I can have a playdate next week. We can pretend to be superheroes.

I feel angry when it rains.

Playing inside is **boring**. I want to run and ride my bike. My parents say I cannot run in the house.

My brother has an idea. We can dance on the rug.

Dancing is fun. I hope tomorrow we can play outside again.

I feel angry when I have to wait. I wish it was my birthday now!

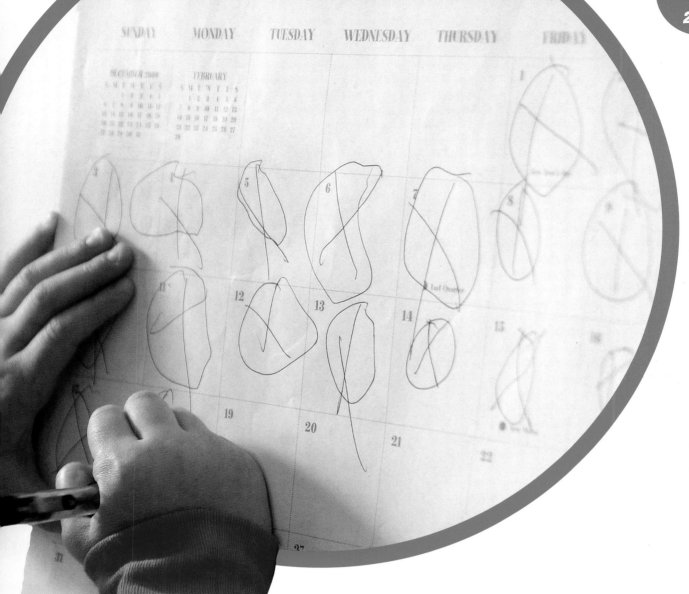

I look on the calendar to see how far away it is. I count the days. I hope the wait will not feel long!

Lots of things can make me feel angry.

But yelling at people does not help. I take a seat. I take a deep breath. I try to be calm.

Words to Know

boring Not fun.

practice Doing something again to get better at it.

superhero Someone with amazing powers.

Index